Diary of a Young, Black

NEG(R)US

MarieAnge Louis-Jean

NEGUS

- **The word comes from Ethiopia, meaning KING.**

- **"N-E-G-U-S description: black emperor, king, ruler…" (Kendrick Lamar)**

For all the little black girls, with words so deep they leave lasting lacerations on your soul, know that your voice is needed. Know this world, this galaxy, is yours, is you. Know that your screams will no longer be silenced, and I hope this book gives you the grace to shout to the heavens, having our orishas parade you to your newfound goddessy.

To me.

LIBATION

AGE 23

I was terrified.

Of?

You.

Poukisa?

What if you hated me for not wanting you before?

You want me now. You love me now, don't you?

Yes.

I am yours and you are mine.

Nothing can ever change this.

We are forever bonded and aligned no matter when we fuss or fight.

I will never leave you. I could never hate you.

Thank you.

How do we begin to return to each other?

You speak as if I left you at some point.

Then where were you all this time?

Patiently waiting for you…

"I will never leave you"… hm.

You simply couldn't see me yet… You weren't ready.

It's ok.

It's ok…

Give yourself permission to cleanse… release.

I pour and say?

Libation.

To you, myself, for honoring your fear.

You may now lay her to rest.

Why must you lay her to rest?

She kept me bound to everyone but myself.

She misplaced my care…

She robbed me of joy.

She made me believe I had no right to choices, to choose me.

Anything else?

I—

Ki?

What if there is nothing left of me once I let everything go?

Then you'll have every ounce of room to be your purest. You get to choose to be someone new, whoever you want.

You've laid fear to rest…

I needed her

For?

Protection.

Are you still afraid?

No.

"Now I'm always smiling!"

Hooking each crease to the edge of earth

Each step stretches me further

To please pleasantly while saying pretty please hoping
to succeed in winning your heart

Cheek bones shall be laid to rest

Little opera, belt your last note.

Exsanguinate

I pour and say

Libation.

No more will I have to bend and break to "keep you".

I lay to rest my need to impress.

I am happy with myself.

Pour and say Libation, now

For the moments you felt unworthy of forgiveness

For the moments you blamed yourself for all mistakes made

Yours or not

Pour and say Libation

For the moments I felt the need to quiet myself

To protect you while simultaneously rushing my demise

For the moments I felt the need to hurt myself for them

Settle for them

Think for them

Be for them

Exist… for them

and never for the benefit of life,

but the continuation of competitive destruction.

They feed on misery

They languish in your desolation

Starve them.

Listening to water seep through my soil

Roots illuminating with each drop

Salubrious river of revivification, floating me

Laying hands on dismembered follicles

Releasing spikes to nestle in each wound

as they burst, trickling new etchings onto my mold

Wrapped in a cocoon of ancestral dauntlessness

Palm rolling severed lives back to never-ending code

We pour and say

Libation.

We pour libation for the woman we once were

For the divine being we are destined to be… and are now.

For the divine beings that came before,

That we once were and still are

We pour and say Libation.

I am complete.

I always have been, and I always will be.

ODE TO 23

Breathe.

That's it.

Wake up every day and decide to breathe

and with each inhale,

Let Loves ocean of luxuriant purification envelope your
heart and spirit.

I love you.

I love me.

I am love.

I am life.

I am EVERYTHING.

I Am.

TO: ME

AGE 22

Sweet, Black Goddess

Sweet, Black Goddess

with hair so coarse you could whip your master, with

tendrils whose slice imitates guillotine.

Rip his lips from that pallid mask

as if shredding to the guitar

because Jimi would have pride for your lack of mercy.

A mold being

Golden Lifeblood of Oshun,

Breath of Oya,

Creator and destroyer like Shiva

Split Earth's core and like Magna with hot magma

we burn through the genesis of shackled expectation

returning to nexus, Mother.

Skin so deep to carry all the hues.

A body made of bulletproof diamond

To reflect and deflect back to your foe.

Sweet, Black Goddess

I know it hurts

to swallow nails like captain crunch

and bandage your overflowing puss,

sludging out like tumor fat excessively regenerating

again and again…

Add a lil brown sugar,

make the bitter milk sweeter to drink.

Don't you see **you**

still blooming into today's hydrangeas

garden growing to an oa-SUS! …

My girl, they pick your ravishing petals

cuz they can't find em' nowhere else

in the universe.

Sweet, Black Goddess

Don't let them see your tears

but also, free them from your pupils

along with every other colorful emotion to ever exist.

Create new feelings of wonder!

Snatch your birthright, **IT IS YOURS**.

Sweet Black Goddess

Don't you know your power?

Don't you know your worth is immeasurable?

Don't you know you're indomitable?

Unmoving, Unshakeable

Unbreakable

THE MOST HIGH

Sweet, young,

Vibrant,

Magnetic,

Wonderous,

Black

Goddess

Stand

the fuck

UP.

AGE 22

Metamorphosis

Women

Walking portals to dimensions

Accordion chasm of pooling euphoria and divination

Make me a world where glossy, glittery black unicorns shoot strawberries from their horns

Taco meteor showers and raining bordeaux caramelized crisp cookies OMG THEY SO GOOD!

Make me a world where money grows on trees (*it already does*) and governments don't exist and when you commit a crime you get put in time-out with your favorite snack and maybe a wonderful book to read and your community service is yoga & meditation 5 days a week

Make me a world where empathy exists everywhere

Make me a world where I'll always see my grams and mom and sisters and brothers smile all the time

Make me a world where hatred doesn't exist

Take me to the moon

I want to see how far the black hole goes

Will it take me back in time?

Will I see God?

Will I see myself?

Take me to the pink dolphin whirlpool where I'll be greeted with snuggly eskimo kisses and we'll swim along the river of swirling, heart-shaped water slides that float in the sky like Pearl's room on Steven Universe

Take me to a world where the sun actually smiles back like in Telly Tubies

Take me to a world where I have my superpowers, laser beam eyes and moving trees with my pinky

Take me to a sea full of stars

I want to sleep in the sky with the constellations

I feel every possible galaxy in all fibers of my being

Take me to the barrier where dimensions cross

I want to see all worlds merge and flow like one embryo

I want to see how beautiful all of this amazing wild ride is

Being a woman is so magical!

I'll go bask in life in my reflection

Catch you later

AGE 22

My ichor

Hemorrhage thicker

Breeds richer

Collects golden lick-or

with fissures that pressure to become bigger

Drink me up

Freshest sap in your cup

Inspires luck

Protects with the most precise, vigorous buck

I'm invincible

Slick visuals

Take yo jugular wit my red goblins and widen your optics

So you know

I am the preeminent

BONDYE!

ZONE BLACK

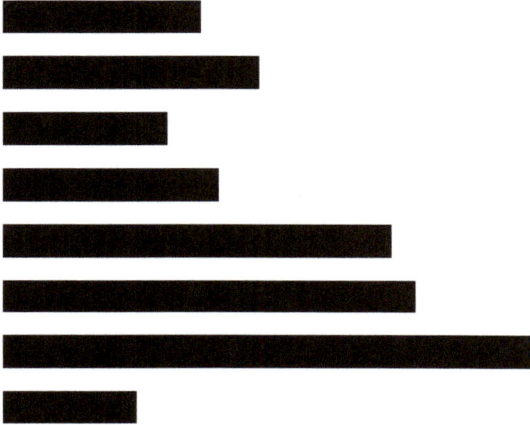

Let acid rain become confetti

And bombs become fireworks

ZONE BLACK CONTINUED
AGE 22

War becomes festival

Pick bones like candy

Concentration summer camps

Jailhouse rock-a-bye baby

On the tree branch

When the wind blows

That twizzler rope snaps

WITHHOLDING

Crooked smile

Crackle face

Dark bags under the eyes

Of an 80-year-old man

I believe he is exhausted

Afraid

His sins he ignored

Crime he did not admit to

WITHHOLDING CONTINUED

AGE 22

Of being black

In Amerikkka

Oh…

To be black

In Amerikkka.

10.JANUARY.2019

AGE 20

Withered

I've stopped

My un-watered psyche has withered into a cesspool

of venomous,

suffocating infection.

I feel the unrelenting clutch of despondency on my heart

I am choked into submission

It's spreading…

Feels like the radiating heat of demons

Toxins crawling from my heart

Pressing

Tightening and traveling down my spine

Paralyzing my existence

I'm exhausted

I crave death.

AS: AGE 20 (10.JANUARY.2019)

Awaiting Wither

AGE 22

Today's the day…

Isn't it?

No?

Cool.

Today's the DAY.

Nope?

NOW TODAY'S THE DAY!

Oh…

I thought you said at any moment, ma.

I thought you said tomorrow isn't promised.

Do I make every moment, take every opportunity

or is this a warning to bide my time?

A target on my back,

at every millisecond.

Keep my eyes forward?

What prize do I win if the game is rigged?

Don't look back

Don't look back

Shit, I looked.

2.DECEMBER.2018

AGE 20

I'm standing

In a white abyss of nothingness

Cold

I'm standing

In a black abyss

Warm

And across I can see myself reaching

With a smile

TO: AGE 20 (2.DECEMBER .2018)

AGE 22

I'm standing

In a white abyss of nothingness

Icy

extracting me from my marrow.

I see my breathe fog up the air

Forming the words "sprint!"

While slowly morphing red tape around my deterioration

Hands punching and pressing from inside out

Extending my fleshy massacre

Bubbling me

Exploding me to become the newest murky mist

Now… I'm standing in a black abyss

Warm

and across I can see myself reaching

with a smile.

Asking me

To love

I am my home,

My haven.

My own savior.

29.JUNE.2018

AGE 20

The veracity of your switchblade tongue is almost
flummoxing

Corrupting my sense

My judgement

I'm blinded by the comfort of home

But smacked and suffocated by the barbarity of your
larceny

Reminded over and over that you are in ascendancy

You took me

You broke me

But what you weren't expecting was for me to recover

And fluoresce brighter than before.

17.MAY.2018

AGE 19

That girl look like she bout' 15 years old by the face

With coffee in hand

Breathing like she has the world on her back.

Maybe she does.

Is she imitating the look of her mom in the early morning

Getting herself ready for the corporate day of sluggish capitalism and hegemonic abuse

Is she for real?

She does have the world on her back.

She is stuck between being an adult and trying to live her childhood.

INSPIRED BY AGE 19 (17.MAY.2018)
AGE 22

Little black girls are hinged in the middle

of transatlantic pole exotic,

or wildin' out lion den, dine in

For your viewing pleasure

but never to simply move without critique

Wrists leaked punching bags

Blackened eyes and blackened smiles,

Black & Mild… mannered, they demand

But be smokey get smoked

Not your mental consideration

8.DECEMBER.2017

AG 19

Submit to your desires

Passions

Your soul's needs and chronic cravings

Breathe into the sonic yanking

Your inner most, ego-centric impulses.

Taste the cherry rose of the innuendo

Feel the warm,

radiating,

writhing drive to be.

To exist

To love

To accept your whole self in your most true self

Living your best

You.

AS: AGE 19 (8.DECEMBER.2017)
AGE 22

Because even at my best

You'll still find something to nitpick

Nap-grip

So fuck it

Fuck you

Fuck yo mama

Yo grandma too

Yo cuh-rusty founding fathers that didn't found shit,

Not even you (AHA)

Fuck all y'all bland ass,

raisin inna potato salad ass,

non-seasonin' asses... I KNOW y'all be hungry!

Dog tongue-kissin', lickin', fuckin',

triflin' incest herding,

Street clothes inna bed nasty ass.

Non-existent culture having ass.

Flat, inverted ass head ass.

Rhythm DIPPIN from you wit ya off-beat, down on the 1 & 3, GOOFY ass.

No washcloth usin' dirty ass.

Burnin' in the sunlight cuz ya stupid asses wanted to walk to the end of the fuckin arctic and have all the melanin froze off them dry ass, tired bones, so now ya dumb asses burn in the sun witcho genetically defective, demonic vampire ass muhfuckas take yo STUUUUPID ass in the house fuck out my face

Thievin ass

Murderin', genocidal, pillaging, pyromaniac ass

Bleached

Etiolated muthafuckas

Y'all need to go back to where YOU came from

19.OCTOBER.2017

AGE 19

I'm in love with my solitude.

My private bubble of magnetic recreation

Unclean unwinding and rebirth

The purest form of myself.

AGE 18

I woke up today and I smelled blood.

It was everywhere.

In my bed sheets,

on my blue painted walls,

in the floorboards and the fireplace.

The curtains.

Carpets.

My clothes…

All of my clothes.

My body reeked of blood.

INSPIRED BY AGE 18

AGE 22

If I sew my heart shut, will I stop breaking from your pain?

If I clamp my spirit down, will my being stop aching for your embrace?

If I lock my soul up, will the numbness become permanent silence?

I'm petrified to open my eyes

I'm tired of visiting the red sea for my daily water

Slowly striding and eyeing the thick, sticky & silky gore

Letting every stroke paint your expired masterpiece on this black vessel of mine

Pretty little raindrop rejoining vast seas

Prints imprinting infamous transference

Replaying transitions which have their breathes stolen away

I raise my hands high to the lord

We thank you for this time

and spring back

Floating & basking in torridity which liquefies me

Calm these cascading ripples

Red is for the blood we shed

but wounds have become so gaping

my back flows like the waterfall of infinite cardinal expansion forming a cape so long,

stretching all the way to the center of dawn

Every spirit snatched too soon glides on my train of slaughter

Don't ever leave me

Don't ever leave us

We won't

But don't you leave us behind either…

AGE 16

The vindictive asphyxiation of bacteria

May be vanquished

By the syringe of art in dream.

INSPIRED BY AGE 16

AGE 22

So I'll dream a dream.

I'll dream so deep it becomes my reality

and so…

It is.

Yes,

It *is* that simple.

25.SEPTEMBER.2014

AGE 16

If the chest caves in

from un-splendidness

Slendermen

Mind vibrations and

jargon from intellectual conversations

of the cotton gin.

Intense suspense,

past lives tackling me with blind eyes.

Ties untied

No binds but I still feel

Unkind

To the reflections in the mirror.

19.AUGUST.2014

AGE 16

Analyzing how I succumb to the way my shoe fits

On my tiny foot

Walking in the grass that leads to the end

Watch the sewage pipes explode

Into a rain of intellectually broken dreams

You can't fix my unstable,

Incarcerated heart.

TO: AGE 16 (19.AUGUST.2014)

AGE 22

I'm still behind

These rusty bars

Cocoa asylum

Where are my keys?

19.AUGUST.2014

AGE 16

Slim thick

slit wrists or at least a thought

That passes on and on

Subjected to society's image of a stable home

With a nice, home-cooked dinner

Kitchen tables aligned

with the framing of a picture resembling the struggles after the renaissance

The anomalous way my blood boils and thins out

As I watch my life get shut down

Indecisive one-mile track

Antagonized by bitter speeches

of why my sneakers can't touch the outside of my front door

I miss my friends

Melancholy birthday balloon

Plants wilting from not getting love from the moon

Biodynamic caramel skin

Infused with shame from words held within

Agateophobia has crept under my skin

Hair follicles have turned into weeds

from an overgrown sunflower garden.

My reflection is shown from the silverware

Upside down faces in the dip of the spoon

Can you see the saltwater leaking from my eyes?

Dry white stains have formed

Bags the size of mothballs

under the pupils of a teenager with amaroidal sweet kisses
from her mother

who desecrated the soul that was a free spirit of rooted
grass beneath waves of time.

As I lay watching the full moon,

I watched as my hands faded

into the abscond light from my favorite suspenders.

They clung to the rack in the back of my closet

My kneecaps have cracks that stretch to Alaska

I have collapsed into the foreboding time warp of a break
down

Maybe I will be ok

After I am done

Wasting out the infirmity

Indisposition for the way

My eyelids droop black paint

My nails dig into what is left of the skin on my head

I have wasted votive love for running

I think I will stop

and have a reparation for my mind

Dead and gone

Wasted.

MIRROR AGE 16 (19.AUGUST.2014)
AGE 22

The anomalous way my blood boils and thins out

as I watch my life get shut down

Indecisive one-mile track

Antagonized by bitter speeches

of why my sneakers can't touch the outside of my front door

Instead of the killer clown, it's my neighbor Sam BO-rown

or my favorite uncle who always gives me the best shoes…

Silent whispers for who not to run to…

And my teacher forgot to lift his hand off my lower back…

And forgot to stop inching lower…

And squeezing…

This form is not mine.

Still written in ink man vs. property

What spin cycle are we on?

Century number 29?

When do we rinse without repeat?

I miss dreaming…

or simply…

Thinking…

of anything other than war.

18.AUGUST.2014

AGE 16

A Girl's Problems All in One Day

Incoherent babbling about my next dress

Slip stitch and dry sex

You put me in a kitchen

After 45 minutes of telling me I'm not good enough

Bewildered by your ignorance

Lousy silence

My shoes have been thrown down

With wires

flat tires

the door slammed and all I could do was choke

I broke

And had been stupefied by more than 20 lies

The mirror cracked

My face has been smacked by

Residuum from a garbage dump

Inside your esophagus

Knife in hand

43

I went from classified

To well denied

To down in the dumps

And the override

Gave my head a nice drumbeat

To dance to

Corpulent body sludge

Not a hot tamale

My vision has faded and now

I can't remember what it is I should be fighting for
anymore

I will walk through the maze

And let the twilight become day

I forgot the date

I forgot my own name

I got swallowed by the daisies and soon enough

They and myself

Forgot my silhouette

TO: AGE 16 (18.AUGUST.2014)
AGE 22

Colorist mutilation

of colorless degradation

of wrapping with bandages

of hiding my charcoal elbows

of bleach eye droplets

get my cobalt vision

with bleach tied knots

if I marry will it seep in?

But I don't want you…

I want…

Can I want?

9.AUGUST.2014

AGE 16

Plastered red steps

You stripped me of my skin and defaced me

I'm scratching and itching at my body

Until brown becomes pale

And blood is emptied of the veins

I tore away at the hairs on my head

Screaming and screaming

Safe was an understatement

Thanksgiving dinners now are

Silent buttocks on couch cushions

The TV is off

The oven is cold

I'm locked in my room because

Kin is now my worst nightmare

Condensation on the glass cup is like

The clocks going tick …

tock…

Let me out

Or just lock me in a basement

And chain me

To the paint peeling walls of hell

I'm not going to talk

I'm afraid.

9.AUGUST.2014

AGE 16

Daddy's Girl

Puppy eyes

Sad whine

Sitting on the couch till 9

Bags packed

Had a snack

Guess it's time to unpack

Fell at the door on the floor

No mat

Hardwood floors

24 hours

Multiple showers

No flowers

They died

Another excuse

Not verbal abuse

But I'm still hurt inside

Drag myself upstairs

Take down my hair

Lie down under the sheets

Wonder why

He never came by

It's cause I will always be daddy's girl

Right?

INSPIRED BY AGE 16 (9.AUGUST.2014)

AGE 22

Daddy's Girl

I had roses in fingers

Ready to adorn your calloused hands

with crimson trickled thorns of endearment and sweat

stitched scars

I had a glass of water to quench your thirst

Ease your fermenting enervation

A towel ready to thrash your condensed,

dripping beads

and yet

Your stride never passed the threshold

As time goes on, disappointment turns anger, turns resentment, turns

Please all gods and universe…

Ancestors!

Let him come home.

Heart thumping so hard it could catapult out my chest

My drooping lids couldn't hold anymore

All I have is the sound

of your constant departure

Will our babies be smooched at entrance by their fathers?

or shall they always be

Remembrance

Emerging from shadows of endless work

Endless slaving

Endless conveyer belt of captivity

You know no rules of fatherhood

Your father's hood taught you to hold the weight of the world

Don't let them pawn you daddy

Sike

Daddy's girl,

the new pawn.

1.AUGUST.2014

AGE 16

Weeping willow tree

Come and find me

In the graveyard

Sulking

She chewed me into pork meat

Mastication

Corruption of a wild sunflower

Face lines pointing down

Eyebrows bent out of shape

I had a recurring dream

That maybe

Earth would regenerate

The cessation came too fast

I've died.

TO: AGE 16 (1.AUGUST.2014)

AGE 22

I dreamt so much of a new world

The new world came

I didn't realize

It wasn't made for me

28.JUNE.2014

AGE 16

Vultures at night

Saints by day

Your virtue

Is not what keeps you away

AS: AGE 16 (28.JUNE.2014)

AGE 22

Manmade morality

False security

You can lay with mistress and wife

Be down low in the alley behind the park

After dark

While sticking soap bars in mouth of spawn

But for me to be openly loving all humans

I'm a sin

Your created abomination

and yet we blindly continue

Sprinting sheepishly like lambs to the slaughter

Awaiting your fabrications,

Rotating judgement

Begging to be cleaned

Lord take these hands of demonic fortitude

I promise to continue to abandon my true nature

Free me of this

So my family can love me again

So they can accept me once more

Even if I have to kill part of myself to do it

Please, cure me

Amen.

27.JUNE.2014

AGE 16

0/zero hours to live and yet we still waste time because when the countdown finally began, we thought we had all these seconds to idly let pass by. And when I got in the car, I turned on the radio. I'd decided I would take a drive and not think of anything. I watched the yellow dashed lines on the road move fast, but my car was going 20 mph. We are now down to 697, 288, 466 seconds left. Next was the park because even though deserted children of the wind still swing on swings and slide down slides with invisibility… BUT I WANTED TO SEE ROME and Italy is told to have the best pizza, but what can you do with 4 hours left to live?! And the sunset is near 2 hours left, shoes still hang from telephone wires… *1½ hours left*! My trunk is filled with nicnacs, and all my tires might go flat, *45 minutes*, so I'll go to the beach and hold my stereo on my shoulder, I'll sing the blues and continue to think of nothing… just nothing. *15 MINUTES*!!! My feet are in the water, where waves are hitting the shore and I know I should have ran to the edge of the earth, my arms high in the sky and I'm screaming GIVE ME MORE PISTACHIO ALMOND ICE CREAM, life is about breathing and seeing and thinking that this is not going to be the end BUT! We have **one-minute left**. **1 minute** to read the last page of your favorite novel, **1 minute** to sing your last song, **1 minute** to dance the last dance, do the scat, make a rap, the indigenous creatures are fed up with this crap! You had **1 minute**… to say sorry or goodbye or simply Hi. **30 seconds**. **15 seconds**. **5, 4, 3, 2, 1**… 0 seconds to live, 0 minutes to live, 0 hours to live, to breathe the last breath. Because when you had the time, just like me in my car, you thought and did…

Nothing.

MIRROR OF: AGE 16 (27.JUNE.2014)
AGE 22

Because when you had the time

Just like me in my car

You thought and did

Nothing.

Now body count counts bodies

Blood is on your hands

freezing

White hands

How does it feel

to finally see color?

20.JUNE.2014

AGE 16

Sometimes we forget what our faces look like

We hide behind

And in-between lines of b.s. that steals away our pride

Stoners beyond boners

Rape and not date

People eat tape strips

and replay that same ole' scene

AGE 22

Welcome to 2021

It's all still replaying

replaying

replaying

replaying

skip

skip

skip

Please skip

Why can't I skip this?

20.JUNE.2014

AGE 16

Soak until a prune

Sweet as a peach

the aroma is dark purple

like

cranberry juice

but the color is lavender

and I looked and watched

bubbles rise to the tub rim

this is a children wonderland

I'm still a child.

DEAR AGE 16 (20.JUNE.2014),

AGE 22

So many moments

I wish I could've held you

Squeezed you so tight that you wouldn't have room to leave my love

Told you to cherish your youth

Kiss your concrete torn thighs and cerise cheeks

Cheer you on to run even faster to your prize

Release inhibitions and don't turn around

Tanpri,

Don't turn around

Keep your pirouettes while you cheese at the limitless

Wish I could embrace & kiss your fragile head

Fill it with softer permissions

Be whoever you want

Even if no one understands

It's ok

Love life and everyone in it fiercely when those around you can't

or won't

BUT!

From a distance…

It's ok you don't know everything now

What you want,

Who you want,

Where you want to be,

Who *you* want to be,

It's ok to not want anything…

But to simply be.

Cradle your optimism

That every art form is yours and it doesn't matter how it looks

Art is everything

THE WORLD IS YOUR OYSTER!

Fear is nothing more than excitement in disguise!

That we're all deserving of love

and love will save the world one day.

SHUT THE FUCK UP YES IT WILL!

Bless your mind for sweet dreams and to keep your honeyed hopes

All of them will come true

You have the magic beans!

Let you know you deserve

All these moments

And more.

Sincerely,

You

18.APRIL.2014

AGE 15

I walk and I walk

She walks and he walks

They walk

We walk

On a rainy day in the middle of nowhere

Is it rain or acid that is falling?

Toxins release into the air

Blinded by the wind

Deaf by idiocy

And we still walk

It's a cloudy day

We breathe unauthentic air

No one would survive

With

Just

Fresh air.

A choke

Silence.

TO AGE 15 (18.APRIL.2014)
AGE 22

We're still suffocating

They took our eyes

They took our minds

Still tugging on heart strings

Hoping one will catch and restart the beat

11.DECEMBER.2013

AGE 15

To mourn

A time to recognize who is gone

The moment of defeat

It's a beaten-in rule that you MUST

Be sad for a person who has died

It's cold to not care, right?

It's inhumane

Sit in the seats of the freezing church

Decorated glass windows with

"your God" and his Mary

An alter and a priest

A dead body and a coffin

A room full of unknown souls

You sit and stare at a closed coffin

You know you have no connection to a dead body

But everyone around you is crying

Saltwater leaking from the faces of complete strangers

In a chamber of short stories

You have a moment to remember

Now it's time to look away

A corpse has no need

A corpse CAN NOT need

Compassion

Nor sympathy

It is only death

AS: AGE 15 (11.DECEMBER.2013)

AGE 22

It's useless to cry, I know…

I feel you as if you never left the seat next to me

Though on another plane

Your essence of sunshine will always motivate me

I still hear your bubbling laugh that made my shoulders moonwalk

Music to my soul I'll never stop vibin'

Your smile so heavily stitched on my own mouth

Sharing your almond eyes and curved lines

Hugs that always brought me home

Smooches and nose nuzzles engrained on my cheeks

The flutter in my heart to radiating heat on my chest

because you crossed my mind and I felt your cuddles

A blanket of the most golden tranquility

Felt your lullaby love that swayed and floated me

and I sprint to my turquoise slumber cloud so I can quickly be sung to sleep

with your heavenly melody…

So I can await your visits

A disco of our most liberated souls

Bouncing off the walls with our hands swinging high and hips stretched as far as they can

Get down girl get down

Hips round and round

Aaaahhh soukee soukee nah

And as I awake to return to present earthly plane

Though I shed a tear

It's only because I miss you so much here

Because I want to hold your hands

and cling to you so you fuse into my flesh

and run down the stairs almost breaking my back to get to your phone call

Blow kisses to you in the phone

Scream down water slides with you

Travel the world with you

Make more memories

Stop taking time for granted

But I grin knowing that your eyes follow me

and your heart creates a veil over my mortal

Keeping me on my path to live fuller and as long as you

How could I ever think you left

When I always feel you

Even in spirit

I am you and you are me.

DECEMBER 2013

AGE 15

A brown hat with lace straps

A white shirt that is now gray

His hands covered in coal

And he breathed

A breath of vigil death

He was aroused by the feel

Mist from the large fountain hit

A face of hard work

A face that burned in the fire

of a flame which turned bodies to ash and ash to dust

The boy sat at the fountain

A beach for the spirits who had no place to go

He sat

And picked at the coins made of copper

Held in his hand

All filled up

It is only what he saw

His own reflection

The coins fly up and it is

Now diamond like rain returns

A rejoice

A new rebel.

TO: AGE 15 (DECEMBER 2013)
AGE 22

Don't celebrate too much

or they'll give us something to cry about

Give us reason for torture

Their punishment is worse than death

Frown a good frown

so you'll see another day

Another day of hell on earth

Burn baby burn

20.SEPTEMBER.2013

AGE 15

I seek it all

The want

The need for attention

For someone to notice

The melanin of my skin

How vibrant and alive it is

In all time

Life goes on with

Events of excitement

With shoes in mud,

Hair in rain

I'm still dancing!

I don't need to be awake

I know I've been seen

There is color.

TO: AGE 15 (20.SEPTEMBER.2013)
AGE 22

They notice that charcoal tint

How it instills their unwarranted, imaginary trepidation

Angst that they'll get too lost in your pools of perception

Terror that they'll recognize themselves

If they stare too long their soul will moan

Groan and siphon the veneer off

Engulf from inside-out

I see your true face stir underneath

Deform in labefaction

Your face stretching the topcoat

Split you open from the middle

Peeling away past sinews as one limb after the other plops

You gush putrefying sludge

Turning swampy green and thickening

Leaching acidic smolder

Neck **krik-**

Arms maimed crackle **-krak**

Face choking on dead skin

Teeth launching out like popcorn

Return them to original form

Breathe

20.SEPTEMBER.2013

AGE 15

In life we ask for forgiveness

No. that's a lie

We demand forgiveness

And then we die

Without a single "yes"

It's no more

You're selfish

And I'm guilty

For being so sensitive

Stopping your heart

You vanished

I'm so sorry

That you needed

Forgiveness

INSPIRED BY AGE 15 (20.SEPTEMBER.2013)
AGE 22

I didn't ask you to speak

I never needed you to say anything

No useless apology

I only ask you stand in the way when they aim to spray

with cased alloy, copper petals

which send me flying to my meadowed haze

I only wanted your shield

But let me keep my air

My channel

Because when you fall

they shriek with textiled grief

But when I collapse,

I'm dragged to the pile with a smile of vengeance

and 4 chambers of misery.

28.JULY.2013

AGE 15

The mind was detached

Deterred and dying

In time.

10.MAY.2013

AGE 14

I walked heel-to-toe

On the train tracks that used to connect

Oh so perfectly

It was nighttime

And no one could see me

Because the bushes covered me like a blanket

Soon enough

I found my face on the tiny pebbles that lay under the tracks

I didn't stay there

I just sink

And sunk and sunk and sunk

Until finally I touched concrete which has now become

Lake Shore Drive

INSPIRED BY AGE 14 (10.MAY.2013)

AGE 22

They had us trapped

The cotton stuck to my skin from Ms. Sun's loving rays

As she drenched my body with the perspiration of my
ancestors' wildest manifestations

To revolt

and bite back

Fight back

But whiplash snapped my cap

Telling me to keep picking

Stand still and keep sticking

Gums attached so my soles are glued

to Satan's irresistible,

sleek,

quicksand

"Salutations

Let me trace my lingo along your gorgeously naked,

succulent nape

draining you of your need to escape

Chillaaaaaax

Blend into my claws grazing your urban, swarthy umber

of refinery

nick you of this poisoned lineage"

Love me like you love your blue pistol

Hug me like you squeeze the trigger

Can I yank you into my bosom and caress you

Clench you close into purgation

Show you peace of mind

How you cock the glock and rifle at my barren chest

Open

Waiting for your return

24.APRIL.2013

AGE 14

I see cracks in the pavement

And broken swings

That just can't

Stop

Moving…

The emptiness of a child

To hold the dandelions

And blow them when the wind is just right

We don't allow the inner kid to keep walking through the grass

Chasing a balloon that just flew away

No.

We shut out all memories

And let dreams become our nightmares

Why not learn to keep running after the tiny things most dear to us?

Why not forget about growing old?

For those who cough up blood in their sleep

And sneeze out muh-cus

I'm sorry

And in that park

with the broken swing that just won't

stop

Moving…

The cracks still lie on the gray pavements

Where street cars drive by

And people ride bikes

But no kids slide down slides

Or move up and down on the seesaw

We

are

grown

We don't want to imagine flying cars

Or wings on our sandals

Fairytales have been replaced by newspapers

When was the last time you rode on roller skates

Or maybe had your first lick of an ice cream cone in a long time

When will we learn that growing old makes us blue in the face

And we've lost our natural glow

Unhang your old sneakers from the telephone lines

Tie your shoes

Put pigtails in your hair

Become a newborn

Once

More.

INSPIRED BY AGE 14 (24.APRIL.2013)

AGE 22

If only our newborn babies didn't have to be sent away in baskets at the river

Flowing into the arms of our "hole-y" creator

Some stories weren't shared fully

Premature to a life unwanted

Emerging with shrieks of remorse for the paradise they've been plucked from

If only our mothers didn't fear for life as much as they pray for it

Hands clasped together as if they've been mutilated shut with barbed wire

If only they could keep their promises to us

and the ones to themselves

To always protect

Always hold us close

Give us the world even though the world was never given to them

and their mothers

and their mother's mothers

though mother herself made it for us to share

Have we forgotten so easily that this world was never ours to claim?

APRIL 2013

AGE 14

UPSTANDER

It's like a wave of

Tied up knots

I saw his knees become tiny pebbles from the ocean floor

He knocked knees and they began to bleed.

His broken bones dropped in its scraps

The junkyard closed its gates

And he lost his eye lids to a bully that lost his cranium

His sleeping mentality

With bandaged knuckles

From all his old boxing matches

He picked his victim up by his ankles

With the words that

Crack you open from the bottom and makes its way up.

Slowly.

Painfully.

I

Was

Running

And my toes helped me jump

And when the bully was knocked down

The victim got up to stand tall

But he stayed

And picked his bully up

And walked away

With his broken-down sneakers

And his knobby knees.

INSPIRED BY *UPSTANDER*, AGE 14 (APRIL 2013)

AGE 22

Pick me up too

I sprinted to be your savior

Your guiding luminosity

Was I nothing more than your stepping stool?

Do I not remind you of who nursed you?

Does my chestnut not evoke nostalgia of your own sculpting?

A door mat to your final destination

Mine is still in this junkyard

Your knobby knees have become my fragmented tomb

A crumpling cave

Dried up

Used.

Abused.

Trial six trillion,

Five hundred eighty-eight billion

Two hundred seventy-nine million

Four hundred twenty thousand

Three hundred and one

and I'd do it again and again…

Just for you.

MARCH 2013

AGE 14

Glorious exhaustion

Incensed in bruises

He disappeared faintly

Nearing strange vigil, but eventually hypnotized

Despised and undeterred

Boarded then twisted

With more bruises and exhaustion to come

Dying away as the crowd sinks in.

CONTINUED... (AGE 14, MARCH 2013)

AGE 22

These are the final expressions he'll see

Distorted and sludging

Blending into one

Riot

On his neck

Am I next?

Maybe this time with me...

They'll make it to 10

26.AUGUST.2012

AGE 14

██████ a smile ████████████

██████████████████

██

Feel my pain as it leaves me

██████████

Tears ███████████████████████

██████ a running stream never ending

████████████ sizzling ██████████

████████████████████████████ skin peeling from my face

██████████████████████

█████████████████████████████████ ████████████████████████

██████ black hole sucking me in

████████████████████ point of no return

██████████████████

██████ clinching on ████████████

██████████████████

▮ need acceptance

██████████████

██ losing air, ████████

█████████████

Grasping ████████████

██████████

█████████████

Deeply hiding away inside

█████████████

██████████

████████████ controls me

██████ engulfs me

████ captured me

██████

██████████

███████████████

████████████

██████████

██████████████

██ certainly ██████

██████████████

██ you see ████████

██████████████
██████████████
████████████
█████████████

██████████████
██████████████
█████████████
███████████

████████████████

AS AGE 14 (26.AUGUST.2014)
AGE 22

I envy you for being so comfy in your body

You bask it in the sunlight in its most bare form

The sun that kissed my strongest muscle to hold strength
from UV

The sun that made my sienna brown skin your enemy

You treat mold with gloss so she shimmers in the blaze

While I sit in the penumbra and pack mine with dust

Hiding from your

(U)nadulterated. (V)iciousness

You bejewel your skin with the brightest bijous

and the wildest flowers from mother

A mother you take for granted

While I tear away at mine

Scorching it in hopes it'll be evaporated off by morning.

Mother I want to be pretty too

You smile a smile of confidence and
twirl your new pretty dress of fine lace
While I pluck away at last year's goodwill
but I'm grateful for anything

You see so clearly where you journey next
and I wonder if I have more paces to take
Have I been granted more time to stroll?
Yes'm massa
Only to the gate
I'll be back before the streetlights come on
Before sundown

You kiss your echo and wish her a great day
While I watch myself atrophy
into worthlessness.
I'm tired

I'm only 14.
What am I so tired for?

22.JULY.2012
AGE 14

Feet touch the surface

Cold like an icy sea

Face stale like a statue

Silk stuck to my body

Lights bright as the sky

Colors shine in the horizon

Heart beating like a drum

Words unable to escape

Tiny steps into my journey

Ready for any obstacle

Running to the finish line

Hesitating to cross

Standing in the center

Reaching for my goal

Almost in my grasp

Caught in the mist

TO AGE 14 (22.JULY.2012)

AGE 22

But the mist was tear gas

Jolting me to

POP POP!

AGE--

A cycle is a circle

A circle is round

A machine moves around in many motions of noise

But if you aren't in sync

You don't think to blink

And your lungs crush

Because you moved ahead

And did not speak

Not once.

CONTINUED… (AGE --)

AGE 22

So, how many times will I muzzle myself

before it's my undoing…

Walking with hands chained behind my back

Fingernails bloodied, broken down to beds of maggots

Ripping layer upon layer

Head locked in a jingle belled box

Stretch my jaws behind my ears and cut my tongue out

Tongs pry opens eyes, scolding

Bloodshot

Fire erupting from sockets like walking Infernals

Don't run too loud

Don't shake too ferociously or Santa will come stuff your throat full

Searing hot coal

Branding your vocal to only be his

Contorted vertebrae by vertebrae

Head between my legs

Eyes rolled back

To exercise leeches

Sucking me to desiccation

Pour molten lava through the rifts

Back blades shredding out

Like barbed wire becoming enlarged and curling over

Foaming from my jaws

Like rabid dog

Rapidly quaking

Rupturing at my existence

14.JULY.2011

AGE 13

WHY

Say you love me

For I am trapped

With this hope

That you will save me

From depression and despair

I dream

That you will rescue me

For you love me

Is this true or not

Please don't forget me

Or I shall be beneath me

For I shall die of pain

Because you said you envy me

And I want to know

Why?

AS AGE 13 (14.JULY.2011)
AGE 22

Have you forsaken me?

I know I'm your strongest,

But please, not for an eternity.

Are you angry that we don't speak all the time?

I barely know you.

But I am you.

Am I not?

Am I not the beauteous image you hoped for?

Was I left in the oven too long?

I thought you were taking your time

But it's more like I left your mind.

I missed your thoughts

I missed you.

For all the little black girls with words cutting them so deep they leave lasting lacerations on your existence, know that your voice is needed. Know that your screams will no longer be silenced, and I hope this book gives you the grace to shout to the heavens and have our orishas float you to your newfound goddessy.

To me.

NEGUS

- The word comes from Ethiopia, meaning KING.

- "N-E-G-U-S description: black emperor, king,

  ruler…" (Kendrick Lamar)

Diary of a Young, Black

NEG(R)US

MarieAnge Louis-Jean

www.ingramcontent.com/pod-product-compliance
Lightning Source LLC
Chambersburg PA
CBHW051818110426
42740CB00056B/143